CHINATOWN
SAN FRANCISCO

CHINATOWN

SAN FRANCISCO

Photographs by Peter Perkins
Text by Richard Reinhardt

LANCASTER-MILLER PUBLISHERS

CHINATOWN San Francisco
Photographs by Peter Perkins
Text by Richard Reinhardt

Copyright © 1981 by Lancaster-Miller Publishers
ISBN: 0-89581-038-7

LANCASTER-MILLER PUBLISHERS
3165 Adeline Street
Berkeley, California 94703
(415) 845-3782

Typography by Jennifer Tayloe
Printing by the Dai Nippon Printing Co.
Design by Wendy Calmenson

Printed in Japan

Map compliments of Jack Chen

Library of Congress Cataloging in Publication Data
Perkins, Peter.
        Chinatown, San Francisco.

        1. Chinatown (San Francisco, Calif.)—Description.
2. San Francisco (Calif.)—Description.
I. Reinhardt, Richard.   II. Title.
F869.S36C476   979.4'61   81-19328
ISBN 0-89581-038-7   AACR2

Downtown San Francisco and Chinatown

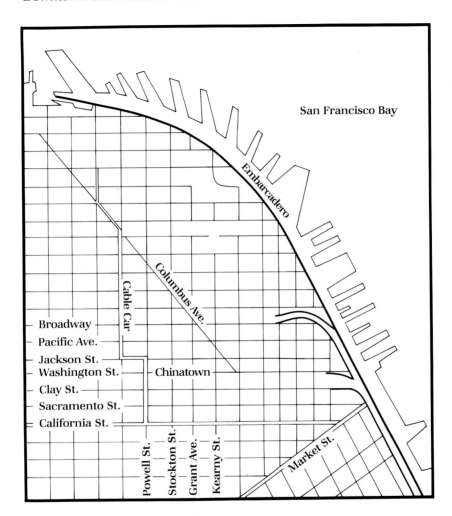

San Francisco Bay

Embarcadero

Columbus Ave.

Cable Car

Broadway
Pacific Ave.
Jackson St.
Washington St. — Chinatown
Clay St.
Sacramento St.
California St.

Powell St.
Stockton St.
Grant Ave.
Kearny St.

Market St.

Of all the American neighborhoods I have ever seen, Chinatown creates the strangest combination of impressions, an incompatible yet indissoluble blend of pleasure, curiosity, and guilt. It is this unlikely mixture of impressions that draws people back to Chinatown long after they have bought their fill of paper fans and incense burners and have permanently satiated their appetite for shark's fin soup. It accounts for the love, the suspicion, and the ambiguity that so many people feel toward Chinatown.

One afternoon a dozen of us visitors were clustered outside the street door of the Lee Family Association, nipped at by mischievous breezes from the ocean. We were watching a man in a white jacket make Dragon Whiskers out of little packets of spun sugar fibers wrapped around a filling of sesame seeds and chopped coconut. Five Japanese businessmen were taking pictures of one another buying Dragon Whiskers. A boy in a baseball cap was trying to persuade his father to go treats. The whole street glittered with the gimcrack, posterpaint look of a carnival midway: This was Chinatown the tourist territory, the amusement zone.

Then, turning the corner, looking for a place that sells take-out *dim sum*, we came upon a narrow lane of such forbidding darkness that we hesitated to go in. A black cat froze in its tracks and stared at us, then darted up a wrought iron fire escape. A gong sounded from a basement stairway, and a thin soprano voice began to sing. Ghosts of old Chinatown rose out of the past, old nightmares of tong wars, opium dens, and hatchet men. This was no facade set up to dazzle tourists. This was Chinatown the menacing, the mysterious.

Farther along, in Spofford Alley, the windows at street level were curtained with sheets of colored calico. Through the open doorways we could hear voices and laughter and the ratcheting whirr of sewing machines. A woman in tight black trousers and a loose green blouse was standing by a doorway, thoughtfully sipping her midafternoon bowl of congee, the thin rice gruel that is so comforting to the Chinese palate and so insipid to the unaccustomed Westerner. A friend came outside to join her in a moment of sweet idleness. The two women turned their backs on the bales of cloth and the piles of unfinished dresses. The friend stood with her thumbs hooked on her waist, massaging her back with her fingertips. She muttered something that made the woman with the porridge throw back her head and laugh. As we walked past, swinging our bags of take-out *dim sum*, the women looked away. Watching them, I felt the separation, the historic wrong that also is Chinatown.

Chinatown is both a place and a metaphor. The metaphor is elusive (we will have to grapple with it later), but the place can be described with some precision. The City Planning Department draws its invisible borders roughly along California Street on the south, Mason on the west, Chestnut on the north, and Kearny on the east. The main street of Chinatown, Grant Avenue, reaches south in a sort of panhandle, connecting the Oriental quarter to the city's retail shopping district. At the point of contact between the two, the boundary is as distinct as a wall. The dividing line is marked by an imperial gate, a much-photographed monument of jade-green tiles, dragons, dolphins, crouching stone lions, and, at the top, four gilded ideograms in raised relief that say: "Everything in the world is in Just Proportion." South of the gate there are banks and cafeterias and luggage shops; north of the gate are The City of Hankow Tassel Company, The Ming Trading Company, The Lotus Garden. Bush Street forms a frontier zone where you can find hamburger counters that serve teriyaki steak sandwiches and a bar called Dillon's Saloon that has Japanese ideograms on the awning.

Most of the buildings in Chinatown are squatty stuccoed tenements three or four stories high. Nearly all of them were built within a year or two after the San Francisco earthquake and fire of 1906. On three sides, this modestly developed area is hemmed in by high-rent real estate—the office towers of the financial district, the retail stores of the shopping district, and the fancy hotels and apartment houses of Nob Hill. On the fourth side, the north, Chinatown has a way of oozing into, and becoming a part of, North Beach, the historic center of Italian life in San Fran-

天下為公

The Dragon Gate on Grant Avenue at Bush Street is inscribed with a plea for justice on earth, written by Dr. Sun Yat-sen, the first president of the Republic of China. A gift of the Taiwan government, the gate was completed in 1970.

cisco. Italians have been moving out of North Beach in recent years and Chinese have been moving in, creating a hyphenate community of Chinatown-North Beach with incredible rents and horrendous traffic.

About 40,000 to 45,000 Chinese live in this nook. No one, including the United States census, can be exact about the figure, because it depends on where and when the boundaries are drawn, and who is asking the question. Anyway, the total does not represent the number of Chinese in San Francisco, many of whom live out in the flat gray avenues of the Richmond and Sunset districts. It often is said that San Francisco's Chinatown is the largest Chinese community outside the Orient, and by certain measures that is true. New York City has more Chinese residents, although San Francisco has a far higher proportion of Chinese in its total population, and they occupy a larger share of space at the center of things. There are perhaps 80,000 Chinese in the city and about 100,000 in the San Francisco-Oakland metropolitan area.

Whatever total you accept, Chinatown is one of the most congested neighborhoods in

Climbing the steep slope of Clay Street (left), the tightly packed apartment houses of Chinatown encounter a barricade of luxurious hotels and residences, rising like castles at the crest of Nob Hill.

North America. It is by far the most densely populated section of San Francisco, which is the second most densely populated city, after New York, in the United States. Chinatown also is a neighborhood of low average income, numerous unskilled workers, countless persons who do not speak or write English, and a high incidence of chronic illness. Chinatown has too many persons per room, too much unemployment, too few parks, and too little plumbing. In short, it is statistically a slum as well as a racial ghetto, although it has few of the unpleasant outward characteristics associated with slums and ghettos. Slums are harsh and gloomy; Chinatown is brisk and bright. Chinatown vibrates with cheerful noise and colored neon. It usually smells of roast duck and pan fried onions, and its balconies are painted green and scarlet.

Clearly, there are several Chinatowns, inconsistent in spirit and appearance. One Chinatown belongs to visitors—non-Chinese, for the most part—who come here for pleasure and who sometimes have the audacity to write about their Chinatown as if it were the only one on the map. Another Chinatown belongs to American Chinese who live elsewhere. Most of the American Chinese who live elsewhere are happy to have escaped from Chinatown, if only because it is so unbearably crowded, but they look on it as a sort of ethnic capital. Anticipating holidays, they scurry knowledgeably through the streets in search of particular herbs and fish and vegetables, and they gather from time to time for family dinners in the upstairs diningrooms of Jackson and Washington Streets—big, barny banquet halls, full of light and chatter and the fragrance of ginger root and garlic oil. The third Chinatown is simply a place where people live. It is not a cultural mecca nor a theme park with a Chinese staff, but an American neighborhood, with a branch library, a health clinic, and a parking problem.

The Chinatown of outsiders like myself is much the largest of the three. It is the province of first-time visitors who wander along Grant Avenue, dressed in lederhosen and murmuring "Schön!" and also the province of Sinophile Caucasians who can speak a few words of Cantonese and can tell the difference between bok choy and broccoli. On the surface, the outsiders' Chinatown does not differ much from, say, Tijuana or Stratford-on-Avon. The clerks at the counters are Chinese (occasionally Japanese or Korean) and the merchandise is mostly from the Far East; but like all towns that cater to tourists, the outsiders' Chinatown mirrors the taste and expectations of its patrons.

The heart of the outsiders' Chinatown is at Grant Avenue and California Street, where a cable car crosses every minute or two with a rattle and a clang and the whirring of movie cameras. On two of the corners are establishments that sell "Oriental fashions." On the third corner is Old St. Mary's Church, which offers salvation and advice. (Its clock is embellished with a warning to observe the time and fly from evil.) On the fourth corner is a wax works museum devoted to such subjects as a costumed wedding in the days of the Dowager Empress, a fortune cookie factory, and a comprehensive torture chamber. The torture chamber is particularly tormenting to those good citizens who have been trying for years to dispel the popular misapprehension that Chinese aristocrats keep thumb-screws and vats of acid in their cellars for the discomfort of drop-in guests.

Old St. Mary's Church, once the cathedral of San Francisco and now a Roman Catholic mission to the Chinese, shares the busy corner of Grant Avenue and California Streets with cable cars, pagodas, and sightseers.

Over the years that I have been strolling the outsiders' Chinatown, the goods in the souvenir shops have gotten more expensive, but the merchants otherwise have shown a commendable Chinese resistance to change. When I walked here as a child, ragging my parents to buy me one of those little wooden boxes that can turn a piece of paper into a penny, the shops on Grant Avenue were chock-a-block with porcelain bowls, brass trays, straw mats, and ivory effigies of Ho Tai, the pot-bellied god of happiness. The shops still are chock-a-block with bowls, trays, and mats, and Ho Tai has not shed an ounce of adipose in a series of cultural revolutions. Lately, however, for the benefit of us repeaters, the shops have added miniature cable cars and T-shirts franchised by professional football teams. It is said that an adroit shopper can find anything manufactured on earth in the shops of Chinatown, and at a different price in every shop. I have not attempted to substantiate this claim, but it would be fun to try.

The outsiders' Chinatown is a succession of tantalizing glimpses: a basement carpeted with canvas mats and hung with an arsenal of bamboo swords and fan-shaped battle axes; a basement lined with tanks of fish; a basement jammed with men and women chopping mushrooms; a basement jammed with men and women sorting snow peas; a basement empty of all evidence of life except a dozen plastic tables, a mah jong set, some overflowing ashtrays, and innumerable decks of cards. In an office building down the street, four flights above the hum of dentistry and real estate transactions, you can peek inside the temple of a furious god, red-faced, black-bearded, glowering upon some distant enemy, far beyond the tins of oil and bowls of fruit along the altar. A light breeze through the window stirs the incense and the breath-of-heaven plants. The custodian looks up and nods but does not leave his chair. Tourists are welcome here. A placard in the hall recalls the visit of President Truman, whose prayers were not ignored.

Down in the lobby a crowd is rushing in to go to the temple or the dentist. A block away you have a glimpse of noodle-makers drifting around like ghosts in a swirling cloud of flour. A batch of noodle dough is slithering like an enormous raw pancake into the open mouth of a slicing machine. The noodle-makers have on white plastic helmets that look like the hard hats worn by baseball players.

The center of the second Chinatown, the one that belongs to the Chinese who don't live here, is Waverly Street, an alley that runs parallel to Grant Avenue and about half a century behind it. Waverly is a street of club houses, the headquarters of the Eng Family Association, the Wong Family Association, the Bing Kong Tong, and other regional service agencies. Tourists wander here safely, but in awe. There are no franchised T-shirts, no toy cable cars. The corner windows of the apartment houses have perky little roofs of turned-up tiles. Dusty philodendrons, festooned with scarlet ribbons, droop in the windows of the butcher shops. There are stores that sell dried lotus, lychee wine, pickled ginger, yenin and chili sauce, giant spinach seeds, salted soya beans, preserved snow cabbages, rice threads, and braised gluten. (The Safeway in the Richmond District sells the same, but the Safeway does not have taped Chinese music nor painted lanterns hanging from the steam pipes.) On Clay Street there is a shop that has on its left, or Occidental, wall a rich display of cigarettes and candy bars and Danish butter cookies, and on its right, or Oriental, wall a chest of drawers from floor to ceiling, stocked with dried sea dragons, ophiopagonis tubers, angelica root, and fritillary syrup. At the counter an herbalist is weighing out dried ginseng on a hand scale. In the window, a pair of velvety antlers swathed in pink ribbon announces the availability of a miracle drug. Powdered antlers go into a costly dietary drink that its users rate as highly as ginseng for bringing back a twinkle to the masculine eye.

If the third Chinatown, the neighborhood, can be said to have a center, it is on Stockton Street. Romantic images of the Mysterious

East die here among the racks of dried, translucent ducks and the bins of pink Dacron stockings, the barber shops and the travel agencies that offer bargain tours to Taiwan and the gambling casinos of South Lake Tahoe. Traffic is impacted in the old fashioned, dental sense, like teeth in a mouth that has too many teeth. Even an aggressive Muni trolley-bus capitulates to the crush of produce vans and gives up at mid-block, hissing irritably. A pedestrian edging around a crate of tangerines suddenly understands the meaning of the statistics about density of population. The statistics mean that there are too many crates of tangerines in Chinatown, too many bins of pink Dacron socks.

On Stockton Street is the headquarters of the Chinese Consolidated Benevolent Association, better known as the Six Companies, the crux of all three Chinatowns. For decades the Six Companies was the government of Chinatown, its embassy to the surrounding world, and some people would have you believe that the Six Companies continues to control the most important Asian community in America from its private council chamber, paneled in dark brown wood, gold leaf, and mother-of-pearl.

Surprisingly, the Six Companies is not an Asian institution but an American one, an accommodation of Chinese immigrants to the sort of life they found in California and to the peculiar ways of Americans. In many respects, the Six Companies is a symbol of the conditions that created and perpetuated Chinatown; and if the Six Companies is no longer the single power, the single voice of Chinatown, the reason is that Chinatown, itself, has grown in power and has found new voices. ☆

Exuberant Jackson Street, bright with Asian restaurants and entertainment, meets a steel wall of business monuments east of Columbus Avenue—the Transamerica pyramid, the chunky U.S. Appraiser's Building, the diamond-hatched Alcoa Building.

Portsmouth Square, a terraced garden with a parking garage tucked under the lawn, is Chinatown's front yard. On sunny days (and foggy ones, too), the Square seethes with action: schoolgirls with bags of sandwiches, codgers supervising one another's game of checkers, mothers with children clinging to their knees. When the Chinese first came to California, this was the plaza of a Mexican pueblo known as Yerba Buena. An historic center of San Francisco, the Square has witnessed rallies, riots, and hangings as well as young romance, old conversation, and ageless family picnics.

St. Mary's Square, once the center of a flamboyant red-light district that scandalized parishioners of the nearby church, is now a fresh-air lunchroom, shared by Chinatown and the financial district. Beniamino Bufano's 12-foot statue of Dr. Sun Yat-sen, done in stainless steel and rose granite in 1937, commemorates the "Father of the Chinese Republic," who lived a few blocks from here before returning to China to lead the successful revolution that overthrew the Qing Dynasty in 1911-12. The tiny park (actually a roof garden) was built in 1950 when the city sacrificed the popular downtown square for a parking garage.

Grant Avenue at Clay Street, crossroads of Chinatown, sometimes looks like the crossroads of the world. Visitors in search of hand-wrought jewelry, teakwood furniture, silk gowns, porcelain, and cloisonné mingle with residents shopping for candied melon, dried fish, and pork dumplings. One of San Francisco's oldest streets, Grant was the main thoroughfare of the Mexican pueblo of Yerba Buena, established in 1834. Known then as Calle de la Fundación, the street was renamed Dupont after the American conquest in 1846, and became Grant Avenue (in honor of President U.S. Grant) following the disastrous earthquake-fire of 1906, which leveled Chinatown.

American Chinese live in many parts of northern California, and their fashions and tastes are as varied as those of other Americans. Most look on Chinatown as a sort of ethnic capital—a place to come back to for family celebrations, holiday festivals, and specialty shopping.

Chinatown's narrow alleys, low buildings, and small shops remind some visitors of an Asian village huddled in the heart of a modern American city. Congestion makes the neighborhood expensive, noisy, and inefficient—but it also creates a comforting sense of community. Some residents never venture outside Chinatown; everything they want or need is right here.

Scalloped awnings, French doors, and decorative wrought-iron grilles give a deceptively European look to the facade of Kan's Restaurant at the corner of Grant Avenue and Sacramento Street. Inside, however, the menu runs to Peking duck and walnut chicken. Chinatown's scores of restaurants range from momma-poppa lunch counters to elegant (and expensive) guidebook selections—and there are good ones at both ends of the spectrum. Although every San Franciscan has a favorite, the best, long-standing recommendation is, "Look for a place where the Chinese truck drivers eat."

Painted balconies along the west side of Grant Avenue between Sacramento and Clay Streets overlook one of the liveliest day-and-night scenes in the United States. When the Golden Dragon or its smaller cousins cavort during Chinatown's frequent festivals, confetti and fireworks rain from the windows. In quieter seasons (as above) the balconies are festooned with posters—in this case, an invitation to attend 6:30 a.m. Easter Sunrise Services in nearby Portsmouth Square, Chinatown's heavily used neighborhood park.

Chinese settlers first came to California at about the same time as American settlers did, and for roughly the same reasons. At the peak of the great gold rush in the summer of 1849, a junk from China entered the Golden Gate and dropped anchor in the bay. Its sails of matting stood out like the wings of a brown moth among the masts of hundreds of abandoned barks and brigantines from Europe, South America, and the East Coast of the United States. Its passengers were equally distinctive.

"They were mostly dressed in the national costume," a young merchant noted in his diary after observing the arrival of a group from Canton. "Peticoat trowsers reaching to the knees, big jackets lined with sheep or dog-skin, and quilted, and huge basket hats, made of split bamboo. The lower part of their legs is encased in blue cotton stockings, made of cloth, and with shoes fully an inch in depth."

Several hundred Chinese, similarly clad,

arrived before the winter rains began. Thousands more landed the following year. Most of them, like the white fortune hunters, pushed on toward the foothills of the Sierra Nevada, where a man with a shovel and an iron pan could sift a few dollars worth of fine gold from a river bank in a day's work. Those who stayed in San Francisco lived frugally by picking up salvage from deserted ships, fishing at the mouth of Mission Creek, or netting shrimps in the tideflats.

Like most immigrants on that wild frontier, the Chinese stuck with their own kind. There was a Chileno camp in North Beach, an Australian settlement near Second and Market Streets, an outpost of New England in the sand dunes to the west. The Chinese clustered a block or two southwest of the town plaza along Calle Dupont, as Grant Avenue was called in those days. Before long, people began referring to the area as "Little China." One of the Chinese opened a restaurant. Another set up a hand laundry—marks of progress in a town that ate standing up and sent its dirty shirts by ship to Hong Kong for a washing and a light starch.

When the American President, Zachary Taylor, died back home in the States, a deputation of Chinese joined the memorial parade in San Francisco. They carried a banner that read, "The China Boys." Afterwards, "The China Boys" presented the mayor with a calligraphed letter, thanking him for inviting them to take part in an American parade. One of the local judges—a white man, of course, —responded with a speech welcoming the Chinese into the community as brothers and equals: "Henceforth we have one country, one hope, one destiny."

But the Chinese, even more than other groups of adventurers, kept to themselves. They spoke a language no one else could write or understand. Unlike the Caucasian immigrants, who came from every part of the world, the Chinese all came from the same place, a relatively small area of Kwangtung (Guangdong) Province not far from the city of Canton in the delta of the Pearl River in South China. Driven from their homes by famine, pestilence, and incessant warfare, they came to California as refugees. Other gold hunters, from other countries, arrived with the same horsemen pounding at their heels, but the Chinese were unique in their destitution, their desperation. They were unique, too, in their steadfast determination to return to their homeland. Staying on as citizens was not in their plans. They hoped to make as much money as possible, save as much of it as they could, and then go back to China.

An elaborate social and economic system for the accomplishment of these ends soon developed in Little China. The men from each geographic district of Kwangtung would form an association (the *huiguan*) that greeted new arrivals, saw to their employment, ministered to their health, and, if necessary, shipped their mortal remains back to the homeland. Men with the same surname also affiliated with a *gongso*, or family association—a fraternity of other Wongs, Chens, Lees, or what have you. For men who craved additional brotherhood, there were *tongs*, voluntary secret societies that resembled the Masonic Lodges, Odd Fellows clubs, *Turnvereins*, and marching companies formed in California by lonely young Caucasians.

To bind the entire community together, the six major district associations formed a federation that served as a kind of legislature

A grocery that boasts of being the oldest and a political club that purports to be the most influential in Chinatown share a narrow space on Clay Street. (Both have moved on since the picture was taken.)

Enticing mounds of oranges, snow peas, and cotton socks lure shoppers to Stockton Street, the commercial backbone of "Chinese Chinatown." Broader and brighter than Grant Avenue, Stockton Street is less attractive to visitors from out of town, but is more important to local customers in search of such services as schools and churches, dentists and doctors, and noodle factories and travel agencies that offer bargain tours to the gambling tables of Reno or Las Vegas.

and court of arbitration. This organization, the so-called Six Companies, assumed responsibility for sponsoring and policing the migration of Chinese workers to California. At that time, most Chinese crossed the Pacific as indentured laborers. A labor broker would lend the immigrant the price of his ticket. After he had found a job, the man would be required to pay back the price of his passage in monthly installments. The Six Companies went surety for each worker, held him to his bond, negotiated with employers to assure a dependable supply of workers and an adequate number of jobs. As early as 1849 the services of indentured Chinese were being auctioned like other property in Portsmouth Square. It was a form of servitude that was not true slavery, yet was close enough to it to permit the opponents of Chinese immigration to argue that a system of chattel labor was taking hold of California.

Perhaps it was the specter of Asian slavery that first discolored the bright promise of one country, one hope, one destiny. Perhaps it was nativist prejudice imported from the East, where the "Know-Nothing" political movement disparaged all foreigners. Perhaps it was a sudden realization there was not enough gold, even in California, to make the whole world rich. Perhaps it was merely the determination of Californians to avoid the problems that had bedevilled the Union—the knots of unassimilated foreigners, the linguistic and religious blocs, the cultural disarray. Or perhaps it was the need of a scapegoat whose sacrifice could bring unity to the other elements of a diverse society.

In any case, the white majority rapidly became disenchanted with the ideal of interracial harmony. The first deliberate note of

discord was sounded in the state legislature. This so-called "Act for the Better Regulation of the Mines and Mining" was introduced in 1850 by a former Texan who had brought black slaves with him to Sacramento. It decreed that only natives or naturalized citizens of the United States should henceforth be allowed to mine without a license. All others would pay the prohibitive fee of $20 a month. Ostensibly, the Foreign Miners' Tax was a barrier against what its author called "an emigration overwhelming in number and dangerous in character." In fact, it was contrived to exploit aliens by forcing them into contract labor for American mining companies. It fell no heavier on the Chinese than on the Mexicans, Chileans, and Australians. In time, it

forced most of the foreigners in the gold country to Americanize, find other jobs, or go home.

But the Chinese remained intractably different. They were absolutely distinctive, not only in coloring, facial structure, and physique, but also in costume. Tenaciously, they held to their quilted jackets and basket hats and to their even more outrageous coiffure, the shaved head and long, braided queue that had been traditional in China from the time of the Manchu conquest. The Manchu emperors had required the Chinese to adopt the Tatar pigtail as a sign of fealty, and it became a mark of Chinese nationality. The loss of a queue signified disloyalty to the emperor.

Californians began to convince themselves that the Chinese had outlandish habits, too. Newspapers reported as fact that Chinese fed on dogs, cats, and rats. When not devouring vermin or household pets, they subsisted on tiny bowls of rice and nauseous morsels of dried fish. They were openly contemptuous of flapjacks, plum duff, and other patri-

otic fare. They were said to worship evil-looking gods in temples reeking of incense and idolatry. Their language, written and spoken, was cryptic: no human being could be expected to master it. Their theaters, their music, their games—all their recreations puzzled the Caucasians. The mildest adjective used to describe them was "singular."

It is safe to say that the growing hostility toward the Chinese did not arise from anything the Chinese had done or were threatening to do. The widespread notion that they were "overrunning the country" was ridiculous: In 1860, they constituted less than one tenth of one percent of the population of the United States. Their offense consisted in being different, and in declining to change. During the decade following the gold rush, only three or four Chinese in San Francisco "Americanized" to the extent of sacrificing their queues. Half a dozen adopted leather shoes and took to riding horseback. Two years after the enactment of the Foreign Miners' Tax, Governor John Bigler, who was celebrated for his sensitivity to public opinion, addressed the state legislature on the continuing need to "stem the tide" of immigration from Asia. Not long after, California imposed a $50-a-head immigration fee on Asians. The fee did not apply to white immigrants. Although this tax was ruled unconstitutional by a federal court, every legislature for several decades adopted further measures to turn away Chinese and make their stay in California uncomfortable and unprofitable. Nor did the courts offer relief: In 1854, the California Supreme Court ruled that the testimony of Chinese, like that of Indians and blacks, could not be admitted in evidence in a case against a white person.

Into this atmosphere of anger and indignity, young Chinese workmen, discreetly assisted by the Six Companies, continued to force their way, seeking their fortunes in Gum Shan, the Golden Mountain. When the easily accessible gold was gone, the Chinese found work on large farms, in quartz mines, in stamp mills. Between 1850 and 1860, labor contractors recruited and imported nearly 62,000 workers from the Canton area. About half of them went home by the end of the decade. They were known as coolies, a word of Hindi origin that means an unskilled laborer. By coincidence, the sounds in Cantonese mean "bitter strength."

In the early 1860s, the Central Pacific Railroad began building east from Sacramento, California, towards a meeting with the Union Pacific, pushing west from Nebraska. Initially, the railroad hired crews of Americans, Germans, and Irishmen. But the Caucasians demanded standard wages, and they often took a job merely to get a free ride to the silver mines of Nevada. Searching for cheap, reliable labor, Charles Crocker, the supervisor of construction, began importing small crews of Chinese.

Crocker was so delighted with the work of his coolies that they came to be called "Crocker's Pets." The Chinese proved to be tough, self-sufficient, and tireless. For $28 to $35 a month (out of which they "found" their own food and shelter), they worked twelve hours a day in mountain snow or desert heat. They had no civil rights, no labor unions, no political champions, and—on a bet—they proved they could lay up to ten miles of track in a single day. At the peak of construction, the Central Pacific employed 10,000 to 15,000 Chinese.

When the transcontinental was completed in the spring of 1869, thousands of Chinese

suddenly were out of work. Some went back to China, to hard-earned retirement. Others took the railroad eastward: the first dispersal of Chinese in America. Most found their way to the teeming little Chinatown on Dupont Street in San Francisco. There they could eke out an existence making boots or brooms, matches or cigars. As brickmakers, the Chinese could take home $25 to $35 a month; as domestic servants, $25; as shoemakers, $4 a week.

The newspapers of San Francisco greeted the Asians with vitriol. They printed cartoons of Chinese with rigid queues and teeth like splayed piano keys, barbecueing dogs, spraying water from their mouths onto clean laundry (which the Chinese did, to dampen it for ironing), and spitting into food (which they did not do). Satirizing this mindless bigotry, Bret Harte wrote a verse called "Plain Language from Truthful James," cast in the form of a monologue by a cheating card-shark who is outwitted by a watchful Chinese:

For ways that are dark
And for tricks that are vain
The Heathen Chinee is peculiar.

To Harte's dismay, many readers took the verse literally. Its ironic tag line, "We are ruined by Chinese cheap labor," became a slogan of anti-Chinese politicians.

A succession of city governments singled out Chinatown for punitive "health regulations." One year the Board of Supervisors, after sending a team of inspectors to survey the horrors of Oriental home life, passed a "Cubic Air Ordinance" that required landlords to provide at least 500 cubic feet of air space for each tenant and subjected the tenants, as well as the landlords, to arrest for violations. Hauled in for sleeping in a stuffy room, a Chinese would have his queue snipped off in compliance with an ordinance compelling the sheriff to cut the hair of prisoners to one inch length. Another measure of public safety and convenience prohibited walking on a sidewalk while carry-

Chinese taste in vegetables runs to leafy, pungent bok choy, crispy wong bok and pe-tsai (Chinese cabbage), and succulent bean sprouts—as well as celery, lettuce, spinach, and other greens familiar to Occidentals. The earliest Chinese immigrants to California imported foods from the Orient: dried oysters, shrimps, cuttlefish, mushrooms, dried bean curd, bamboo shoots, duck livers, and chestnut flour. Many Oriental foods are now produced here, not only for Asians, but also for a growing clientele of appreciative Caucasians.

ing baskets at the end of a pole that rested on one's shoulder, the usual practice of Chinese porters. Later Boards of Supervisors contemplated restricting the Chinese to a small area off Clay Street or, alternatively, transporting them across the county line.

A few years after the completion of the railroad, a national depression, aggravated in California by two years of drought, drove the general level of wages almost as low as the pay scale for Chinese labor. Unemployed miners and farmers drifted into San Francisco. Hundreds lined up each morning for relief work at $1 a day. Thousands lounged on street corners, joining the idle hoodlums whose only occupation was picking on Chinese. A jobless man, gazing up at Nob Hill, could see there the conspicuous new mansions of the very railroad owners who had imported coolies to do the work that white men had scorned—and now would gladly have accepted. The connection between unemployment, exploitive capitalists, and "Chinese cheap labor" seemed all too obvious.

A rabble-rouser from Chicago came west to invigorate the masses. At a series of outdoor meetings in the sand dunes near San Francisco's unfinished City Hall in the summer of 1876, one James F. D'Arcy, the organizer of the Workingmen's Party of America, put the blame for the slump on the most convenient target, the Heathen Chinee. After a few weeks of D'Arcy's sermons, the mood of the city became so touchy that the Six Companies sent a cable to the government of China, urging a voluntary halt to migration.

What the Workingmen wanted, however, was not a respite but a permanent shield against Chinese competition. Earlier campaigns to exclude Chinese immigrants had been frustrated by provision of the Burlingame Treaty of 1868, by which the United States had guaranteed the "inalienable right" of Chinese to come to America. The Workingmen's Party promised to nullify the Treaty and, in anticipation of that, to make life unbearable for the Chinese in San Francisco.

The Party's first success was in electing a mayor who proposed to nag the Chinese out of town with taxes, curfews, and other annoyances. With that encouragement, D'Arcy drew 5000 cheering, howling whites to an anti-Chinese rally the following summer. A few days later, a mob gathered at the docks of the Pacific Mail Steamship Company, where immigrant Chinese customarily disembarked. The mob set fire to some sheds, threatened to burn the piers, then swept uphill to Chinatown, smashing windows, looting stores, beating Chinese merchants and hanging them to lamp-posts by their queues. Gangs of hoodlums raged through Chinatown for three days. The mayor called in the Navy, which landed a force of armed marines; and a self-styled "Pickhandle Brigade" of volunteer militia turned rioters away from the wharves.

A new agitator arose in the person of a 30-year-old Irish teamster named Denis Kearney. Kearney's gift of mild eloquence, refined in Sunday afternoon debates at the Lyceum of Self-Culture, ripened into croaking, shrieking demagoguery in the cause of Chinese exclusion. He cursed the "rich hell-hounds" of California. He screamed, "The Chinese must go!" One tempestuous evening he led several thousand men up Nob Hill, where he harangued them to "lynch the railroad magnates" while bonfires crackled on the pavements surrounding Charles Crocker's mansion.

The Workingmen's Party, swept along on

a current of rebellion, dominated a state constitutional convention the following year. Sections of the new constitution would have excluded Chinese immigrants from entering the state and penalized corporations that employed Chinese. At the next general election, the ballots of every political party in California carried the words: "Against Chinese." In San Francisco, 40,030 voted for a petition to prohibit Chinese immigration. Only 229 opposed the petition. The Chinese, of course, were not asked for their opinions. They did not have the right to vote.

The "Chinese Question" overshadowed every other political issue on the West Coast. Although California was strongly Republican, the voters gave six of the state's seven electoral votes in 1880 to the Democratic Presidential nominee because the Republican Party had taken a moderate position on Oriental exclusion. Four years later, the state returned to the Republican Party because the Democrats appeared to equivocate on the Chinese issue.

Faced with such consuming passion, the Congress of the United States passed a Chinese Exclusion Act in 1882 that effectively nullified the Burlingame Treaty and banned immigration for ten years. Re-enacted several times, modified and restated, the Act ended the importation of Chinese labor for more than 60 years. Immigration was limited to real or putative relatives of Chinese already in the United States. The Chinese population dwindled, and a strange peace settled over California. Fear of Asian labor continued to haunt San Francisco, and politicians, editors, and labor leaders could always rouse their constituents by dredging up the Yellow Peril; but the nightmare of fire and riot had ended.

The Chinese, insulated by their deeply ingrained customs, withdrew into their ghetto, giving substance to the baseless accusation that they were incapable of adapting to American life. They lived crowded together without hope of relief or escape. Except for a few doughty missionaries, no outsiders showed an inclination to ameliorate the vile living conditions, the opium traffic, the prostitution and gambling that prevailed in this depressing slum. Instead, white San Franciscans encouraged tourists to visit Chinatown, sniff in disgust, shiver in revulsion, and assure themselves that the Chinese were incorrigibly bad subjects.

The ritual evening tour began with a walk (guided, of course, by a plain-clothes police detective) through murky streets and fetid alleys. Next, there would be a meal in a Cantonese restaurant—"Pale cakes with a waxen look, then giblets of you-never-know-what, maybe gizzards, possibly livers, perhaps toes." After supper, a stop at a joss house, a few minutes of bewilderment at the Chinese theater, an uninformed encounter with Chinese music, and finally, an opium den. Tourists dropped in at opium dens as regularly as they now visit certain North Beach night clubs on the After-Dark bus tour.

Around the turn-of-the-century, an Episcopal minister from Albany, New York, was treated to a tour of a Baptist Church, a newspaper, and a school before proceeding to the opium den, where a frail old man lay on a wretched bed and smoked for the enlightenment of people from Albany. His intake was said to be fifty pipefuls a day at fifty cents a pipe, the funds supplied by charitable visitors.

"Bishops and clerical and lay deputies felt this was a rare opportunity to study heathendom," the minister observed, "and I am sure all went away from this strange spot thanking God for our noble Anglo-Saxon civilization, as well as for the knowledge of His Revelation."

Chinatown became America's favorite slum. Charles Hoyt's musical *A Trip to Chinatown* (1891) ran for years in New York City. It depicted the Chinese quarter as a spooky playground for rich, white San Franciscans with such names as Wilder Daly, Isabelle Dame, and Rashleigh Gay. In popular literature the Chinese were "inscrutable," "moon-faced," and "sinister." They were believed to wallow in gruesome crimes and unspeakable vices. They had, in fact, reached the bottom of their history in America.

The discipline of the Six Companies deteriorated. Fraternal tongs controlled the neighborhood, thriving on prostitution and gambling. The tongs employed "hatchet men" as bodyguards and professional murderers. In the course of their work, the hatchet men would extort protection money from merchants and carry on blood-feuds with rival tongs. They went in for knife-throwing and showdowns in dim doorways. Tong wars gave a vicarious thrill to readers of the *Police Gazette.* The victims were all Chinese.

Precisely at this time, when the reputation and expectations of the Chinese were ludicrously debased and they seemed doomed to waste forever in a noisome ghetto, Chinese children, a few at a time, began to enter public schools. Young men adopted western clothing. Shopkeepers learned English. Gradually, over a generation or two, the Chinese abandoned the idea of returning to their homeland. Whites began to accept the notion that a citizen might be both American and Chinese.

World War II made allies of the United States and China. In the glow of new friendship, President Franklin D. Roosevelt signed a measure repealing the exclusion acts, permitting the naturalization of alien Chinese, and setting a modest yearly quota for Chinese immigration. It was the first of a number of separate acts that opened doors to Chinese women, students, refugees of revolution, and even "paper sons," who had obtained entry slots illegally during the decades of exclusion. This form of restitution climaxed in October, 1965, when President Lyndon B. Johnson signed a new immigration act at the foot of the Statue of Liberty. Under the provisions of this liberal act, thousands of Chinese have come to live in the United States. Most of them pass, at least briefly, through San Francisco's Chinatown. ☆

Baskets from Hong Kong are typical of the multimillion dollar import trade between Chinatown and the Far East. With the easing of longstanding restrictions on trade with the People's Republic of China, goods from the mainland have joined those of Hong Kong, Taiwan, South Korea, Japan, Malaysia, and India on the shelves of Grant Avenue shops. It has been estimated that at least a tenth of the Chinese in San Francisco are engaged in the import-export business.

Surrounded by friends and family, Chinatown civic leader H.K. Wong hosts a banquet of classic regional dishes at the Empress of China's rooftop restaurant. Ranged around the dazzling centerpiece (a winter melon filled with shark's fin soup) are Peking duck with steamed buns; prawns Hunan-style; Hong-sui (whole fish) cooked in the style of Fukien and Kwangtung; steamed broccoli; Szechuan beef; minced squab in an iced lettuce cup; "Flaming Young Quail"; crispy-skin whole chicken with green onion bread; steamed rice; Peking glazed apples; dried fruits; and Chinese candies.

The bikeshaw, a motorized, North American adaptation of the leg-powered jinrickshaw and pedicabs of the Orient, offers footsore travelers a breezy ride through streets and alleys where automobile drivers dread to roam.

A finely drawn line, in finger painting as in hair brush calligraphy, is a mark of perfection in Chinese art. Contemporary artists in many fields (sculpture, ceramics, painting, photography, and dance) show their work in major exhibitions at the Chinese Culture Center on Kearny Street; and one of the finest collections of Oriental art outside the Far East is displayed in the city-owned Asian Art Museum in Golden Gate Park.

The ancient and elaborate art of Chinese herbal medicine uses more than 3000 substances, brewed into infusions that are occasionally rather tasty, but more often are not tasty at all. A single prescription from an herbalist may call for a dozen ingredients, and a well-stocked herb shop offers five or six hundred of the popular varieties of leaves, barks, seeds, roots, resins, nuts, fruits, and flowers. Sometimes a bit of powdered deer horn or a morsel of dried seahorse goes in as well, to give the patient added strength. Measured and mixed in proper proportion, herbal medicines are said to cure most of the ills of mankind—or, at any rate, to cure those that are curable.

The triple-tiered temple of finance at 743 Washington Street (left) once served as the CHina exchange of Pacific Telephone and Telegraph Company. A staff of 20 young women, bilingual in English and Cantonese, handled all calls to and from Chinatown. Considering that scarcely any of the customers knew or used phone numbers, the operators did a splendid job until dials and automatic switches replaced them in 1949, and Chinatown's most celebrated landmark (built in 1909) became a branch bank. The scholar above presides at the Chinatown branch of the San Francisco Public Library, one of the most heavily patronized branches in the system.

Wall newspapers are a tradition from the mid-Nineteenth Century, when irregularly published broadsheets served the first immigrants with news from China, shipping lists, commodity prices, and religious sermons. Papers flown in daily from Asia now circulate briskly in Chinatown, along with such American-based publications as Chinese World, Young China *(founded in 1909 by Dr. Sun Yat-sen,)* Chinese Pacific Weekly, East West, *and* Chinese Times, *published by the Chinese American Citizens Alliance.*

Survivors in an underground economy, Chinatown's street peddlers set up business in seconds, and change premises without formal announcement. At least a quarter of the adults in Chinatown are traditional shopkeepers. The Chinese operate an estimated 5000-6000 business establishments in the San Francisco Bay Area. Clearly, these statistics do not include one-tray or brown-bag retailing in shops without walls.

Small garment factories, each employing about 25 women, are the principal industry of Chinatown. Hidden behind calico curtains in the street-level shops of Powell Street, Spofford Alley, and Pacific Avenue, the factories are almost indistinguishable from neighboring apartments where the workers live. Like San Francisco factories of a century ago (when virtually all clothing that was manufactured on the Pacific Coast was Chinese-made) today's shops tend to resist unionization, licensing, and laws regulating minimum wage, maximum hours, and child labor. But among them, the 200 or so shops in Chinatown provide a livelihood— or part of one—for as many as 5000 women and their families.

An outsider wandering Chinatown can find this story, more or less as I have told it, in the museum of the Chinese Historical Society. It is told there without rancor, and with a certain quiet pride and simplicity that is characteristic of the American Chinese. That the story should be told at all by the people of this reticent community is evidence of profound changes in Chinatown. The Chinese have always been reluctant to talk about themselves and about their experiences in America. Now that they are speaking up, they are discovering an immense reservoir of beauty and courage and sorrow in their buried past.

Until very recently, the Chinese in America have had to share their place with various racial stereotypes, notably the demented houseboy who goes by the name of Wong O'Leary and talks English of the Missee-No-Likee variety, and the insensate Dr. Fu Man Chu, whose long black mustaches dangle unappetizingly from his nostrils and who seethes with an ungovernable urge to put slivers of bamboo under the fingernails of his acquaintances.

It was a surprise to many Americans a few years ago when the usually quiet folk in Chinatown took exception to the filming of a new Charlie Chan movie on grounds that they were fed up with being type-cast as Confucian philosophers. It mattered not that most people thought Charlie Chan and his breezy, American-born son were likeable chaps. The point was that the Chans were not quite human. American Chinese, like other people, have decided that they would rather be depicted as human beings, subject to such human frailties as boredom, anger, hatred, and love.

Out of this search for history, this demand for identity, a harmless myth has developed, to the effect that most American Chinese are descendants of the sinewy laborers who built the transcontinental railroad. This is not literally true, of course, any more than it is literally true that most white Americans are descendants of the pilgrims who left England in the 17th Century to escape religious persecution. All the same, there is a spiritual truth behind the idea, as there is to the idea that all Americans are heirs to the Puritan tradition of New England. The truth is that the Chinese, from the time of their first immigration, always have been important contributors to building the United States. Although the ghetto of Chinatown still exists, a symbol of segregation, the Chinese have been moving out of it into all types of work and every level of academic and financial achievement. Their accomplishments have been far greater than their limited numbers would warrant.

Chinatown is changing in other, more visible ways. The city dug a parking garage under Portsmouth Square and turned the grassy slope that once was Chinatown's front lawn into a messy roof garden. High rises are crowding Kearny Street. Pagoda-like towers and upturned eaves multiply along Grant Avenue. There are more signs, more ice cream cones, more savings and loan associations. The Chinese telephone exchange, a site of mischief in the days of Charlie Chan, has closed its switchboards. Its building is a bank, and a call to China is like any other call, a string of numerals. The Chinese Playground offers courses in Kung Fu twice a week.

Chinatown has burst its boundaries. Rents were never higher. There is a new Chinatown on Clement Street, and Chinese families live in the suburbs, barbecueing T-bone steaks on Saturday night, planting marigolds, hauling boats to Clear Lake to water ski.

Along with getting bigger, Chinatown has become infinitely more complicated. The census bureau estimates that about 2000 Chinese join the population of the city every year. Many of them are from northern or eastern China. These F.O.B. (Fresh Off the Boat) Chinese are of a different culture. They speak Mandarin instead of Cantonese, and many of them do not know English. They have never heard of sweet-sour sauce or the Six Companies. They favor Mongolian lamb and hot-sour soup from Szechwan. Their children do not get along well with the children of American Chinese.

It is difficult to foresee the outcome of this ferment. At worst, it could lead to a renewal of segregation, a return to the mentality of the old Chinatown, the city-within-a-city. As Chinatown bumps against its neighboring

districts, points of irritation appear. Will these become matters of contention between races? Or will Chinatown become what so many Chinese and other Americans have longed for, a zone of peaceful contact between China and the West?

San Francisco often has advertised itself as a gateway between North America and Asia. The claim has never been stronger than in this era of improved relations between the United States and the People's Republic of China. If San Francisco has become, in fact, the meeting place of cultures that it aspires to be, Chinatown inevitably will become the principal showroom of Asian art and commerce and civilization in the Western Hemisphere.

For too many years, Chinatown symbolized rejection and captivity, a rejection and a captivity created and perpetuated by fear. If Chinatown should come to symbolize acceptance and freedom, civility and culture, much of this unhappy past might be forgotten—or, if not forgotten, remembered only as a prelude to a bright destiny. ☆

Festival time in Chinatown calls for cadence drums, embroidered silks, and dancing dragons. The noisiest and brightest holidays are Double Ten (October 10), the anniversary of the Chinese Republic, and Chinese New Year, the mid-winter celebration of a new lunar year. Twelve animals preside over the successive years of a cycle dating back to 2637 B.C.—the dog, boar, rat, ox, tiger, hare, dragon, serpent, horse, ram, monkey and rooster. All are welcomed with food and fire crackers by several hundred thousand excited human beings, all of whom are, at least for the moment, Chinese.

Miss Chinatown USA, an unabashedly commercial extension of the ancient rites of Chinese New Year, gives Chinese communities throughout the West a pleasant excuse for banquets, pageants, fashion shows, and ticket sales. Along with general housecleaning (Dah Faw Hom Muy), bill paying, and fraternal reunions, New Year's now occasions kung fu exhibitions, art exhibits, walking tours, folk dancing, cooking demonstrations, concerts, and civic luncheons.

The Golden Dragon with a camel head, deer horns, rabbit eyes, cow ears, serpent neck, frog belly, carp scales, and hawk talons dances on the sturdy legs of three 22-man teams, drawing extra energy from a generator truck, cages filled with fireworks, and the ministrations of an official "dragon teaser." Built in Hong Kong of papier-maché, velvet, silks and bamboo, the reigning dragon is one of dozens brought from China over the years to grace a succession of traditional festivals climaxed by the two-week New Year celebration in late January or early February.

Brilliantly costumed and highly stylized, Chinese theater came to California in the Gold Rush, and has changed little since that time. One important innovation: women's roles are now (usually) played by females.

Chinese art and crafts—some genuine treasures, some obviously manufactured for cheap commerce— crowd the shops of Grant Avenue. A few residents resent the proliferation of tourist shops, which they say have replaced neighborhood service businesses, but city officials smile on Chinatown's thriving tourism, a major contributor to San Francisco's most important industry.

Chinese immigrants in the 19th Century erected shrines in California to the dieties that had particular appeal to lonely pioneers: Kuan Kung, the ruddy-faced god of war and peace, literature and valor; Pei Ti, the god of the north; Kuan Yin, the goddess of mercy; and T'ien Hou, the queen of heaven and goddess of the seven seas. Several temples are open to visitors, notably the Kong Chow Temple on Stockton Street and the T'ien Hou Temple in Waverly Place. Diverse in religion as in speech, the Chinese also worship in Buddhist, Protestant and Catholic churches and in a temple that combines Buddhist and Taoist belief.